A CALMER SUTRA

Frank Dickens

A CALMER SUTRA

timewarner
books

A Time Warner Book

First published in Great Britain in 2002 by
Time Warner Books

A CIP catalogue record for this book is available
from the British Library.

ISBN 0-316-86053-0

Designed by Janet James
Printed and bound in Italy

Time Warner Books UK
Brettenham House
Lancaster Place,
London WC2E 7EN

www.TimeWarnerBooks.co.uk

When renewing an old acquaintance it is customary for the gentleman to allow the lady to open the conversation with a subject of her own choosing...

It is written that should the woman desire an explanation it is the custom for the man to provide an immediate response...

If one of the partners does not achieve full satisfaction by an Act of Congress it is wiser to say nothing...

DON'T REPROACH YOURSELF — EVEN IN YOUR PRIME YOU WERE ONLY AVERAGE IN THE SACK.....

It is unwise for a man to press the woman for the answer to a question, for sometimes that answer is not what he wants to hear...

M usic can be employed to assist and add to the enjoyment of an Act of Congress...

Before taking part in an Act of Congress it is of benefit to both parties that they be relaxed and comfortable...

Regrets should not be dwelt upon, for their shadows lengthen with the passing of time…

REMEMBERING YOU AS YOU ONCE
WERE, YOUR WAISTLINE COMES
AS A SHOCK FROM WHICH I DOUBT
I WILL EVER FULLY RECOVER.....

An element of danger can sometimes enhance a meeting but the woman should take heed before she proceeds too far along this path...

S ometimes it may be necessary for the man to assist the woman in remembering tender moments from the past...

During an Act of Congress care must be exercised, since passion takes no heed of the physical condition of either participant.

A lady should not appear too garrulous, lest her loquacity prove against her...

B efore entering into an Act of Congress it is not recommended for the man to indulge himself in self gratification.

Servants should be reminded that their first duties are to provide a service and should therefore not be in any way presumptuous...

IT'S NONE OF YOUR
DAMN BUSINESS WHY
MY HUSBAND IS
TRAPPED IN THE
CHANDELIER, BUT
IF YOU MUST KNOW
WE WERE INDULGING
IN SOME CASUAL SEX...

S ometimes the man should admit that the sands of time, as those in a hastily assembled hourglass, do not ever pour evenly...

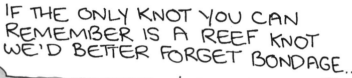

Occasionally an element of surprise will inject something new into a meaningful relationship...

I t should be noted that music, reported to be the food of love, is sometimes not enough and occasionally something more substantial is needed...

Sometimes it is advisable for the woman to think before she speaks.

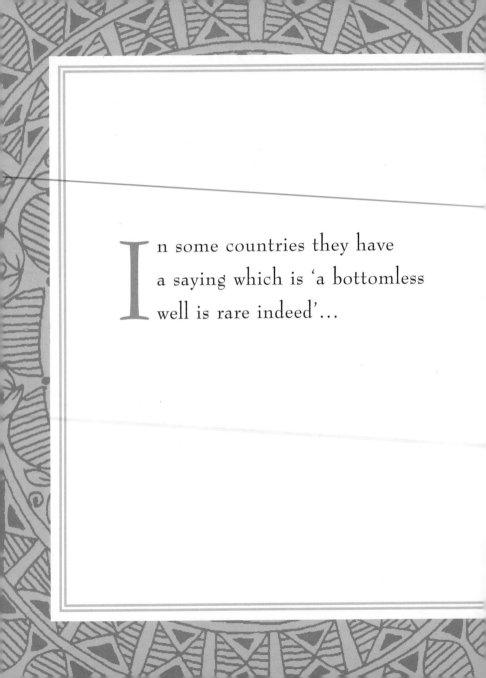

In some countries they have a saying which is 'a bottomless well is rare indeed'…

It is unfortunate for the man that a cruel and heartless woman, if so willing, can terminate an Act of Congress by affecting a temporary ailment...

Humour can enhance the Act of Congress, but care must be taken that the mood is not lost through excess…

There are occasions after an Act of Congress when traces of passion remain. Care must be taken to ensure that it is better if only fond memories are left.

It must be remembered that great care should be taken when an animal is brought onto the scene.

It is permissible for the man to be aggrieved at the woman's lack of enthusiasm after a successful Act of Congress...

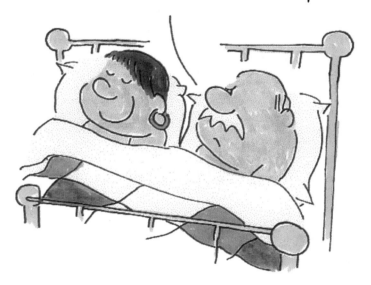

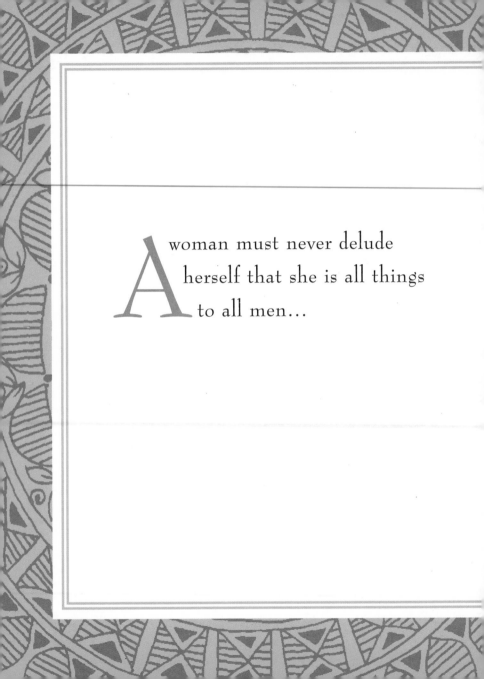

A woman must never delude
herself that she is all things
to all men...

A chance remark, unexpectedly overheard can sometimes cheer and delight ...

Feelings and emotions
expressed in earlier meetings
should be repeated as often
as possible, though the passing of
time may well affect the faculties of
one or both parties...

Sometimes desire can be recreated by discussing past memories with an old acquaintance of the same sex.

It can sometimes jeopardise a relationship if the man suddenly discovers there is more to the woman than he supposes.

It is sometimes necessary for one partner to remind the other that life goes on...

The man must realise that the woman is not as patient as the male and take this into account when arranging a meeting.

There comes a time in the life of the man when he needs not only a place to lay his head, but an attentive and listening ear...

Sexual awareness can be aroused before an Act of Congress takes place by covert glances and titillating conversation over a light meal...

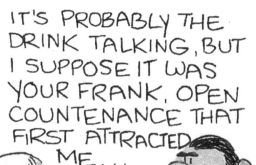

Sometimes, as a token of her affection, the lady will present the gentleman with a small gift of her own making...

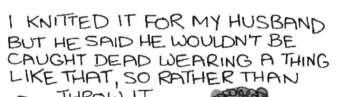

I t must be remembered that a
desire to indulge in the
Act of Congress can sometimes
take a partner unawares and care
should be taken to ensure that the
practicalities of life are not
jeopardised by a sudden impulse...

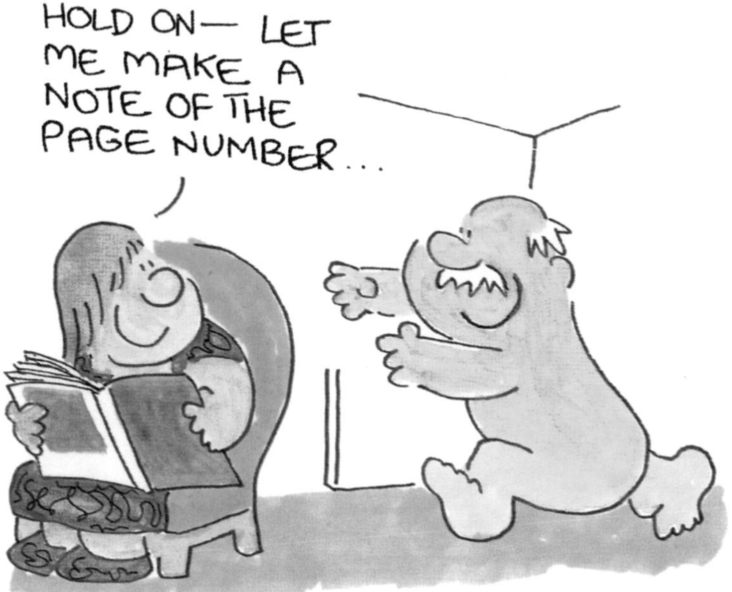
HOLD ON— LET ME MAKE A NOTE OF THE PAGE NUMBER...

It is essential for the preservation of family life that matters pertaining to the Act of Congress are kept from children lest their young minds be too soon corrupted...

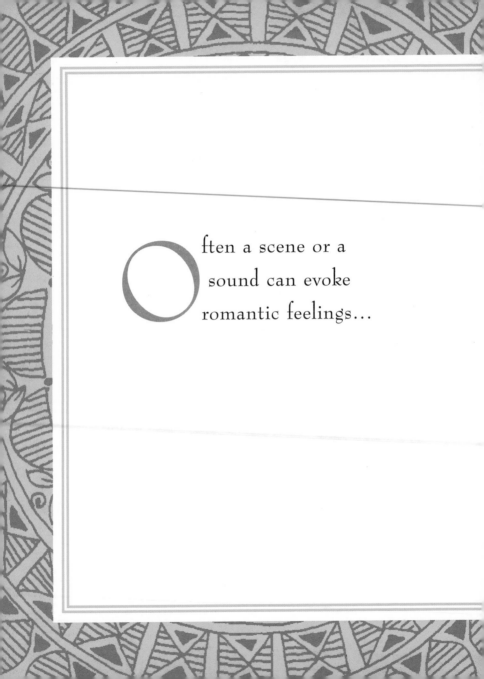

Often a scene or a sound can evoke romantic feelings…

One must learn to ignore the often facetious comments of those in a less fortunate position than one's self...

It is said that sometimes the thrill of the chase can be as pleasant and stimulating as the capture itself...

The art of harmonious sexual congress is sometimes dependent on the trust the one has with the other...

It is sometimes difficult for the man to control his basic emotions, and when necessary the woman should remind him of this...

I t shall be that before an Act of Congress, the man should try to adhere to the romantic ideals ever present in the female.

It is foolish to underestimate the importance of religion in a relationship between a man and a woman...

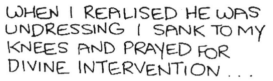

A simple question can sometimes change a relationship and care must be taken in the phrasing of same.

An Act of Congress must be pleasant and rewarding for both partners, but sometimes one requires assurance...

I t is said that recollection, like
the flavour of fine wine savoured
and remembered, is equally as
refreshing...

The guile of the man resulting in the lady succumbing to his charm, the man should waste no time demonstrating further accomplishments...

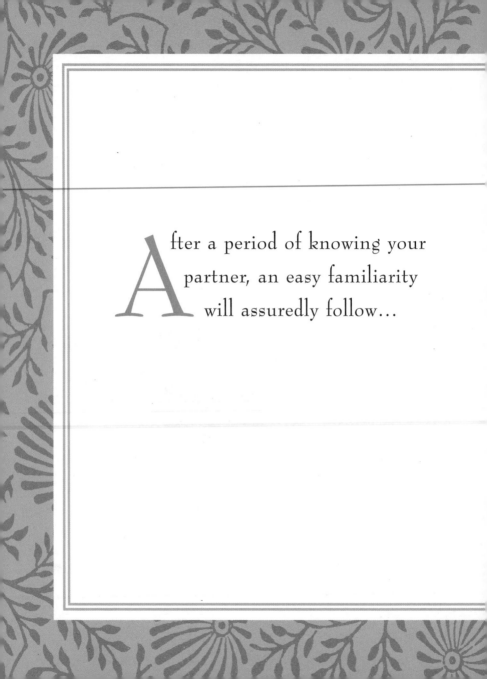

After a period of knowing your partner, an easy familiarity will assuredly follow…

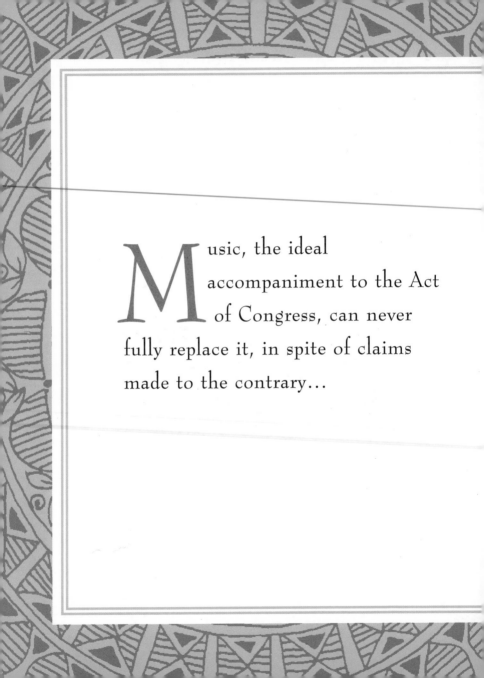

Music, the ideal accompaniment to the Act of Congress, can never fully replace it, in spite of claims made to the contrary...

I t is meet and proper that
questions of conscience must
sometimes enter into an
Act of Congress.

Sometimes in the company of strangers it is proper and acceptable for the woman to profess ignorance of custom...

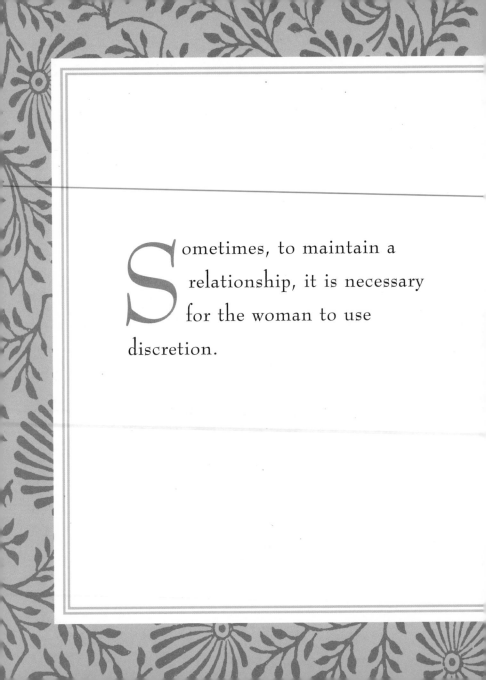

Sometimes, to maintain a relationship, it is necessary for the woman to use discretion.

A sudden jolt can remind the complaisant man that there are two sides to every coin.

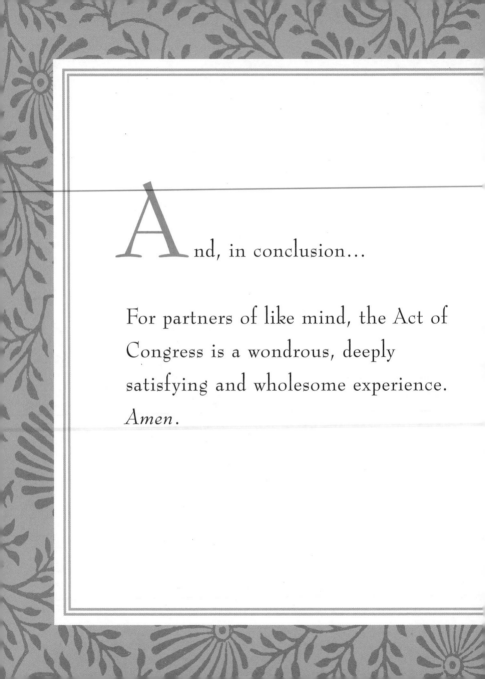

And, in conclusion...

For partners of like mind, the Act of Congress is a wondrous, deeply satisfying and wholesome experience. *Amen*.